Foreword

This book was truly an amazing experience. This project allowed me to involve my entire family. My wife Joscelyn and our three daughters Anastasia, Christina and Isabella all played a big role in this book. Bringing Ollie to life was such an incredible journey. Thank you for giving Ollie a voice.

I started Scoring Goals for the Community in 2017 to give back to local charitable organizations and causes within our communities. Over the years Scoring Goals for the Community has grown and helped so many in need. In August of 2023 we introduced Ollie as the new face of the organization and to connect with our youth.

There are so many people to thank who were instrumental in making Ollie a reality. John and Tasha from Phantom Express, Joel from Munimentum Inc., Dominic from The Crupi Group, Laura from Laura McBride Real Estate, Chris and Rima from The Marc Group, Anand from Ronin Group, Gary, Nadia and Crystal and the rest of the team from MVS Design, Jay McChord and Trevor Claiborn.

To my parents who have always believed in me and have stood beside me through the years. This past year was especially tough, but we had each other to get us through it.

To the De Sousa's. Steve, Tina, Elenna and Alexia. Thank you for your ongoing love and support.

To the Vrysselas family for always encouraging, supporting, and believing in me.

To my "Ollies", Nick Argiropoulos and George Dinan. Thank you for bringing so much life and energy into the character.

Thank you to the Dinan, Loureiro, Butler, Tovich, Lund, and Connery families for all you have done for us.

To my Kiki. You will always be my inspiration and I know you'll continue to be there for me, watching from above. Not a day goes by that I don't think about you and miss you. I love you.

Sotirios (Sam) Daskalopoulos
"Scoring Goals for the Community" Founder

In loving memory of
Lisa "Kiki" Daskalopoulos.

Scoring Goals with Ollie
Written By:

Anastasia Daskalopoulos,
Christina Daskalopoulos,
& Isabella Daskalopoulos

Hi! My name is Oliver, but my friends call me Ollie. I am six years old and for as long as I can remember, I have always loved to skate and play hockey.

After school today, my hockey team has their first game of the season. I think I hear my mom calling so I'm going to head to the kitchen for breakfast.

Breakfast is my favourite meal of the day. My mom and dad always say it is also the most important meal for growing kids like me.

This morning my mom made us blueberry pancakes with maple syrup. Mmmm...Even our pet cat Harvey likes to join us for breakfast every morning.

After eating breakfast, I always remember to brush my teeth, so I don't get cavities. I make sure to make my bed and clean up my room before I leave for school.

I can't wait to see all my friends who ride on the bus. This year: Charlotte, KiKi, Sheldon, Trevor, Nicole, and Benjamin are all on the school bus with me.

When I got on the bus it was so loud, I bet everyone is just as excited as I am for the first day of school. I can't wait to meet my new teacher, Ms. Keys. She is a new teacher at our school this year. I wonder if she found the classroom yet.

When I got to school, I decided to go into my classroom to see if Ms. Keys needed any help. She was already there and asked me if I could put all the name tags on everyone's desk. This will make it easier for her to remember our names. I was glad to help.

Once the bell rang everyone knew it was time to go to class. We all took our seats and got ready for the lesson to begin. Ms. Keys asked everyone what they did over the summer break, and everyone was eager to share their stories.

During recess my friends and I were so excited about tonight's hockey game. David was telling us about how his mom and dad had bought him some brand-new goalie equipment for this season. He says it matches our uniforms perfectly. David's mom and dad also happen to be the coaches for our team.

As we were all lacing up our skates, everyone was trying to guess who was going to score the first goal. I really hope we win tonight because that would be so much fun. Dougie said he is going to try and score a hat trick. Then coach John and coach Tasha came into the dressing room and told us it was time to get out on the ice.

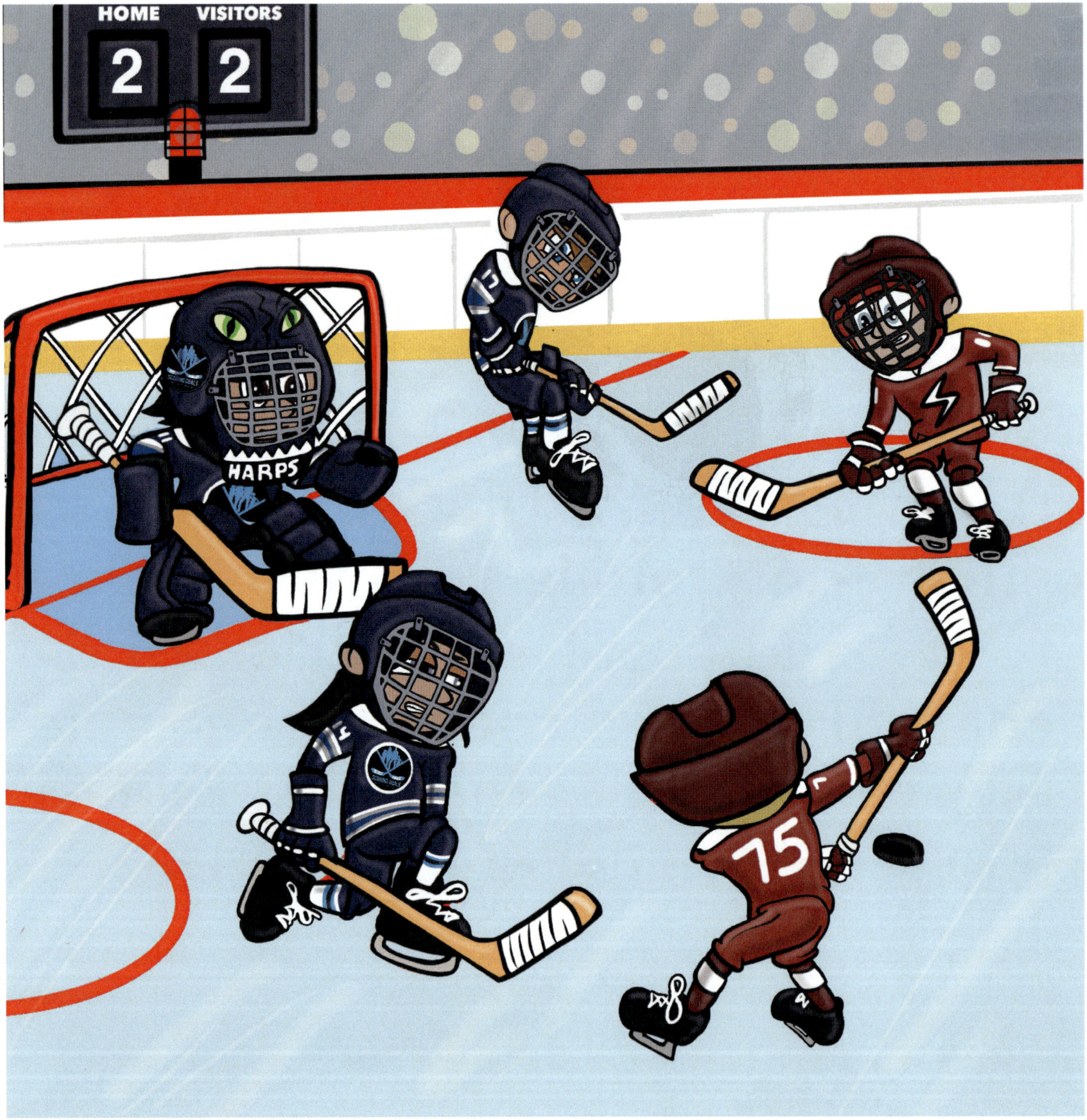
HOME
VISITORS
2
2
HARPS
75

The score was tied 2-2 late in the game. Dougie had 1 goal, and Kiki had the other goal for our team. Everybody was starting to get nervous when all of a sudden, the other team got the puck in front of our net with just five seconds left. We saw the player on the other team wind up to take a shot. We all did our best to get in front of it and tried to block the shot.

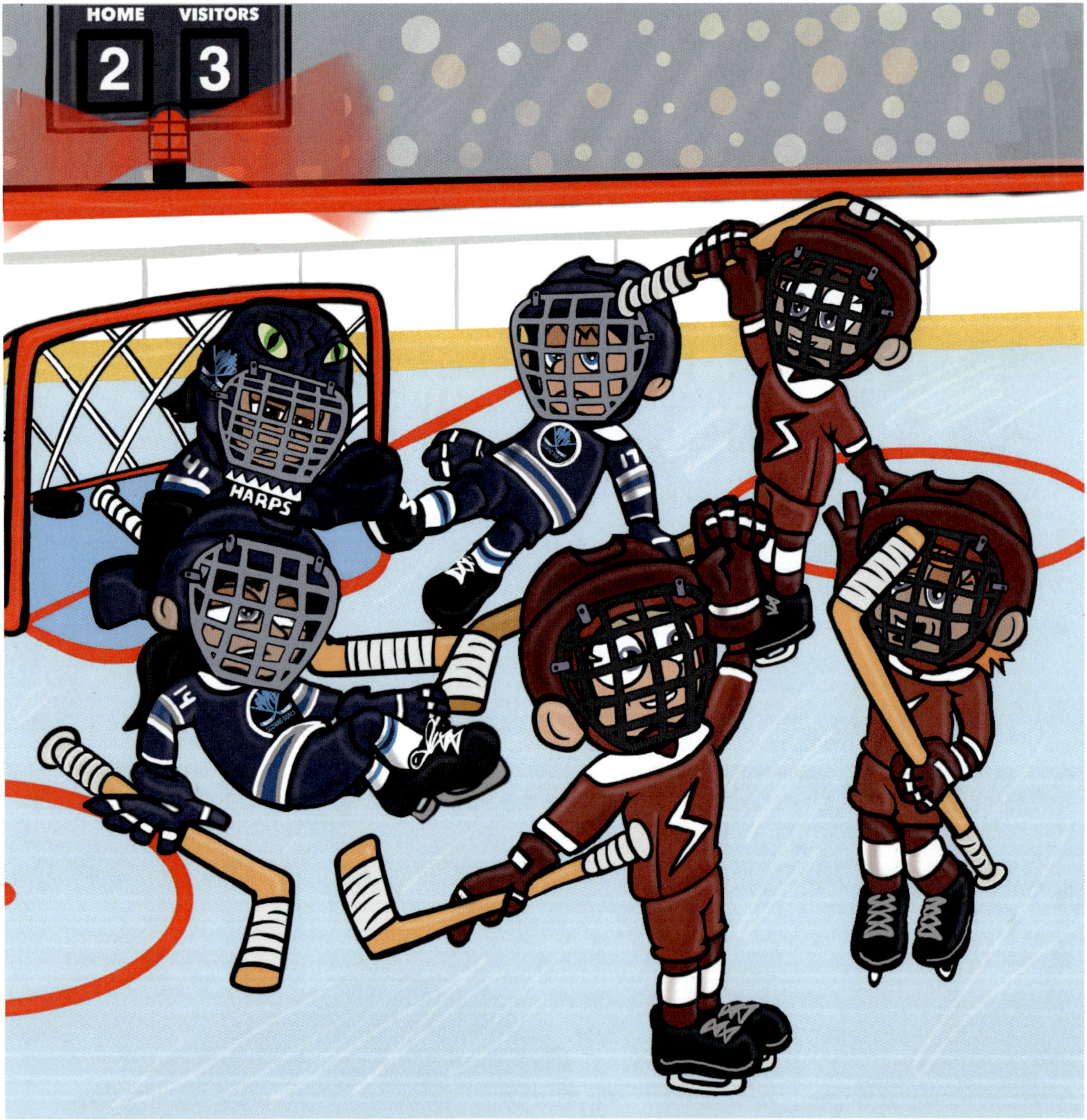
HOME
VISITORS
2
3
HARPS

Unfortunately, it was too late. None of us were able to block it and the puck slid into the back of the net.

We ended up losing the game 3-2. The other team was so happy and celebrated in front of us.

After the game, in the dressing room, everybody was sad. That's when coach John and coach Tasha told us how proud they were of how we played and told us they were taking us out for pizza to celebrate our good effort.

We were so hungry after our game we could not wait to eat some delicious pizza. We talked about some of the amazing saves David had made, the great goal Dougie scored, and how hard KiKi's shot was when she scored her goal.

I hope you all enjoyed my story. Always remember that even though you may not win every game, make sure you have a lot of fun, as that's the most important thing. Spending time with your friends and teammates is truly what sports are all about. See you next time.

THE END!

Ollie's Friends

Sheldon	George	Charlotte	David	Tina
Caroline	Jay	Ollie	Theo	Elenna
Jake	Nicole	Miles	Kiki	Dougie
Jackson	Valentina	Benjamin	Trevor	Alexia

SCORING GOALS FOR THE COMMUNITY

 ALLSTARS

ROOKIE CARD

KIKI #14

ROOKIE CARD

OLLIE #17

ROOKIE CARD

DAVID #41

ROOKIE CARD

DOUGIE #86

ROOKIE CARD

JAY #13

ROOKIE CARD

TREVOR #84

SCORING GOALS
for the community

scoringgoalsforthecommunity.com
Scoring Goals and Helping Build a Better Community

Manufactured by Amazon.ca
Bolton, ON

37795503R00021